THE BATTLE OF LINCOLN FAIR

Its Causes and Consequences

Researched and written by Ellie Lowe
Illustrated and designed by Faye Kingsford

First published in 2017
© Tucann Ltd 2017
All rights reserved

ISBN 978-1-907516-40-5

TUCANN LTD
Unit 9 Blackthorn Way, Business Park, Five Mile Ln,
Washingborough, Lincoln LN4 1BF
www.tucann.co.uk
01522 790009

.Early Lincoln.

Four years after the Roman invasion of Britain began, approximately A.D. 47, the Ninth legion reached Witham Gap, the modern day North Kesteven. The first name allocated to the settlement was the Roman Lindensium or Lindum, which is an adaptation of the British Lindon, meaning 'place by the pool'. Their main camp was based on the modern South Common, but the Romans also built a military stronghold on the crest of the hill which developed into a walled colonia, the highest rank of Roman city.

Lindum's walls were originally built to enclose 41 acres of land, but as the colonia grew it overflowed its designated limitations and was extended downhill. The upper roman enclosure and original city walls later became the Bail, whilst the lower area became the Medieval City. During their occupation of Britain, the Romans left a great legacy of roads, building two crucial highways that intersected Lindum.

Ermine Street comes north from London, and Fosse Way follows a course from Exeter, through Bath, Cirencester and Leicester to Lincoln. The Roman city grew powerful through trade due to the key transport links of the highways and the River Witham.

Their occupation lasted four centuries, but the collapse of the Roman Empire meant the Colonia was abandoned around A.D 395, although it is possible a small settlement remained. By the early 7th century there was an Anglian civic government of the city, which implies that an Anglo-Saxon population took control of Lincoln for a period of time. Between the late 9th and 10th centuries the region was controlled by both the Danes and then English in rapid succession as they both fought for the land, until the Danish King Canute decisively took the city. During this period Lincoln prospered again from its Roman Transport system and became a hub of trade.

.Roman Map.

.Key.

- ■ Ermine Street
- ■ Fosse Way Street
- □ Watling Street
- ▨ Dere Street

Important Roman roads constructed by the Roman army.

.The Norman Invasion.

A fter the relative stability of the Roman era, Lincoln like the rest of the country was constantly on edge, pulled from pillar to post by invading armies. The Anglo-Saxon King Edward the Confessor had succeeded Hardicanute, who had died following a drinking party at the marriage of one of his thanes.

Edward the Confessor, priest was responsible for building Westminster Abbey

Edward had spent the early part of his life in Normandy where he became deeply religious, almost a monk, and took a vow of celibacy. As a result of this when he married the daughter of Godwin of Wessex, Edith, they were to have no children. Edward quarreled with Godwin, his father-in-Law and had him banished from the land. Furthermore, by favoring Norman advisers at court, the King angered the Witan, a council of English Noblemen.

In 1052 Godwin returned to England with his two sons commanding an army, forcing Edward to reinstate him into society. Following Godwin's death in 1053 he was succeeded by his eldest son, who became Harold of Wessex, the most powerful and loyal nobleman in the realm. Harold was a soldier who took part in many campaigns; in 1063 he invaded Wales and devastated the population by killing all adult males in his path. He was shipwrecked in 1064 on the coast of Ponthieu, from where he was delivered to William of Normandy.

Both being soldiers, Harold accompanied William into battle against Conan of Brittany. It is claimed that he swore an oath of allegiance to William and promised him his support for the Crown of England, following which he returned home.

Edward the Confessor had become content to build Westminster Abbey in London, and left the Witan to run the country. So when the childless King died in 1066, it was this group of English Noblemen that appointed Harold of Wessex to take the crown.

There was jealousy in the family, his brother Tostig along with the King of Norway had invaded the North of England, hence King Harold II had to move fast to seize the throne. His army marched from London to York in four days to confront the Vikings at the Battle of Stamford Bridge near York on September 24th 1066. At about the same time William of Normandy had landed his army at Pevensey Bay. Again King Harold II had to lead his army south and ignored advice to leave someone else to command the battle which was to ensue at Hastings. On the 14th October 1066 the two armies met and after a fierce encounter with the English wall of shields holding off the Norman Cavalry and infantry, King Harold II was killed.

King Harold II of Wessex

.The Battle of Hastings.

The illustration is based on the bayeaux tapestry an embroidered cloth commissioned by Queen Matilda, William the Conqueror's wife. King Harold II being defeated by the Norman forces of William the Conqueror at the Battle of Hastings. He was shot in the eye.

'William the Conqueror'

William the Conqueror

Following the Norman invasion Lincoln was transformed into one of the largest and most important cities of Medieval England. According to the Domesday book of 1086 it had a population of around 6,000, which is a large number by medieval standards. Crucially, William I transferred the 'see' of Dorchester to Lincoln in 1072-73, making the city the capitol of the largest diocese in England which roughly ran from the Humber to Oxford and encompassed everything south. This led to William instructing Bishop Remigius to oversee the building of Lincoln's famous Cathedral, which following setbacks would be finished and consecrated by 1280. The Cathedral was a political statement as it inspired awe in anyone who looked upon it, and showed the Normans were a force to be reckoned with. William also commanded the construction of the Castle in 1068, on the crest of the hill in a prime position overlooking the River in the South and the Valley of the Trent to the West. It was strategically situated between the two major Roman highways; Fosse Way and Ermine Street. Such routes were depended on for trade, therefore making Lincoln an extremely influential location. During this era the wool trade was a crucial facet of the English export economy, and Lincoln produced the majority of its wealth from its famous long wool sheep.

William the Conqueror's seal.

In 1087 William the Conqueror died, he had four sons and bequeathed England to his harsh third son William Rufus II. Needless to say that he was not mourned when he was killed with an arrow through the lung while out hunting deer in the New Forest during July 1100. Henry I was the fourth son of William the Conqueror and was accompanying his brother on the hunting trip. Following the King's demise, he quickly travelled to Winchester to secure the treasury and his dead brothers wealth and to claim the throne.

William II was a very hard ruler and was described thus within the Anglo-Saxon Chronicle,

'He was very harsh and fierce in his rule over his realm and towards his followers and to all his neighbours and very terrifying. Influenced by the advice of evil councillors, which was always gratifying to him, and by his own covetousness, he was continually exasperating this nation with depredations and unjust taxes. In his days therefore, righteousness declined and every evil of every kind towards God and man put up its head. Everything that was hateful to God and to righteous men was the daily practice in this land during his reign. Therefore, he was hated by almost all his people and abhorrent to God. This his end testified, for he died in the midst of his sins without repentance.

.St Hugh.

After the murder of St Thomas Becket, King Henry II persuaded Hugh, a young French noble and monk to come to England to become head of the Carthusian monastery at Witham, Somerset which Henry decided to build as a reparation for his conscience of the crime. The building work was failing and it was Hugh who stepped in and got the project moving. In 1185 an earthquake severely damaged Lincoln Cathedral, the Bishops office was vacant and the Cathedral Council and Canons choose Hugh as their new Bishop on 25th May 1186. Bishop Hugh of Lincoln was consecrated on the 21st September 1186 and Hugh was responsible for beginning the restoration and enlargement programme that continued into following centuries and made the building into the magnificent architectural feat that exists today. Lincoln was the largest Diocese in England at the time of Bishop Hugh, he ruled over an area from the Humber to the Severn estuary. He was a dedicated Bishop who travelled throughout his Diocese representing the Pope in matters of state. He was also well know for his caring attitude for the sick, children and the persecuted. As one of the most prominent English Bishops, Hugh acted as a diplomat in France on more than one occasion, firstly for King Richard and later King John. King Richard the Lion Heart is reported to have said of him. 'if all the prelates of the Church were like him, there is not a king in Christendom who would dare to raise his head in the presence of a bishop.'

He died on the 16th of November 1200, and both the English King John and the Scottish King William acted as pallbearers as his body was carried from the Gilbertine monastery now known as St Katherine's up to the Cathedral for his funeral. Following his death, in 1220 he was canonised as the patron saint of swans, shoemakers and sick people.

'The Anarchy'

Robert was Henry's elder brother who upon returning from the Crusades tried to seize the English crown, but failed and instead proceeded to rule Normandy. Robert was a wasteful inefficient king and many Norman Knights invited Henry I to come and take Normandy back unto the English crown. Henry responded by leading an army to the duchy, and was victorious in the battle against his brother.

Henry I

There were celebrations in France involving a great deal of alcohol whilst the men were waiting for the ships to carry them back to England. King Henry was offered the use of a new vessel named 'the White Ship', but declined the offer. However, his younger Knights wanted the best and most up to date transport, therefore accepted the invitation and continued the party. Stephen of Blois, one of the intended passengers apparently suffered sickness so badly that he could not sail. Monks arrived, it is said to bless the vessel but they were turned away.

Matilda

On the 25th November 1120, 'The White Ship' sank near the Normandy coast, and among those who drowned was William Adelin, the only son and heir of the King, Henry I. Facing a potential crisis of succession, Henry nominated his daughter Matilda as heir, but following his death in 1135 heavy opposition meant the throne was taken by Matilda's cousin; Stephen of Blois. The war that followed, known as 'The Anarchy', was waged between family members. Matilda invaded England in 1139 to take the crown by force, and simultaneously sent her husband Geoffrey of Anjou to conquer Normandy.

The English and their Norman masters had a reputation for wild parties and drinking alcohol. The Norman court tried to establish some discipline and etiquette to court life and under Henry II a knight of his court named Daniel of Beccles wrote a 3000 line poem laying down the rules of expected good behaviour. This became known as the 'Book of Civilised Man'

edieval Lincoln was a bustling hub of trade and finance, among the wealthiest towns in England it was second only to London in terms of importance. Fire was a constant risk as most buildings of the time were built from wood, and in 1123 the town was devastated by a blaze that destroyed many houses. In 1157 Lincoln was granted a charter that gave certain rights to the townspeople, making it independent and henceforth the richest citizens elected twenty-four men to form a council and rule the city. From 1206 it also had a Mayor, who was considered the first citizen and took the highest precedence. The wool trade led to a height of prosperity during the twelfth and thirteenth centuries, as the river Witham provided a prime route for exporting goods over to Flanders and from there into Europe. In 1291 Lincoln was made a staple port, which meant it was one of a select group that could export wool, further adding to its prosperity. The city also became known for its cloth, and 'Lincoln green' was famous across the country, worn by the likes of Robin Hood. It had a thriving Jewish community of which the most famous was Aaron the Jew, and there is architecture still existing today that demonstrates this. The Knights Templar was a Christian military order that was formed following the First Crusade, and owned many estates throughout Lincolnshire which served to finance their activities. Overall the city was a hive of activity, attracting interest from every angle, which led to its direct involvement in the Barons war and the culmination of the Battle of Lincoln.

The young knights partying after their sucesss in the land battles turned away the monks who had come to bless the 'White Ship' before her maiden voyage.

A short way from the shore the White ship flounded on rocks and the drunken crew and passengers drown.

The Battle of Lincoln, known as the Joust taken from Historia Anglorum

In 1141 King Stephen's forces were besieging Lincoln Castle when they were attacked by Matilda's army, led by her half-brother the Earl of Gloucester. This battle is known as the Joust of Lincoln, a violent and bloody battle, which ended in Matilda's victory and the slaughter of Stephen's supporters. King Stephen was captured, but due to opposition from the public Matilda was never crowned. In 1148 she returned to Normandy, now ruled by her husband, leaving the campaign in England to her son Henry II who eventually inherited the crown following Stephen's death in 1154.

It was Henry II who in 1155 granted Richard de la Haye the constableship of Lincoln Castle alongside all the lands of his father, Robert de la Haye. His father had inherited this position and wealth through his wife, Muriel, who was the daughter of Colswein, thought to be the very first constable of the castle under William the Conqueror.

Henry II

An effigy of Nicolaa de la Haye at St Michaels Church, Swaton, Lincolnshire.

Upon Richard's death the position was inherited by Nicholaa de la Haye. Her first husband William Fitz Erneis died and she then proceeded to marry Gerard de Camville. Both husbands carried on the work of Constable, and while they were away the duties fell back to her and she carried them out very effectively.

King John is said to have visited Lincoln, and she attempted to

9

hand the keys of the castle back to him as she considered herself old. The monarch held her in high esteem and due to her loyalty he refused to accept her resignation. In 1191 she had held out in the castle for one month when the castle was besieged.

.William Marshal.

In 1147 a fourth son was born to John FitzGilbert, Marshal of King Stephens Court. FitzGilbert had changed sides to support Matilda's claim to the crown, which led to him being besieged by Stephen, and when captured he surrendered his five-year-old son William as a hostage. FitzGilbert reneged on the promise and the child was threatened with death as punishment. FitzGilbert, his father could not care less about the boy saying that he could always have another son. Stephen could not bring himself to kill the child who was to grow up to become a vital player at English court, William Marshal, Regent of England and Earl of Pembroke. Throughout the Medieval period men were usually identified by a lordship, place of birth, or residence. But William chose to take the family name 'Marshal', despite his elder brother holding the formal title of royal-master Marshal. We know him as William Marshal today as he chose this name, perhaps considering that it may be remembered. At the age of thirteen, William travelled to the Castle of Tancarville in Normandy, determined to train in warfare and become a knight. During his apprenticeship he would have mastered equestrian skills, castle and siege warfare, weaponry, and battle tactics. In 1166, Marshal was knighted in a ceremony and proceeded into his first battle almost immediately. It is clear that from this point onwards he chose to forge his own way, and this path was consistently tied with the Crown of England.

.The Angevin Empire.

King Henry II was a descendent of William I, which gave him the birth right to rule both England and Normandy. He married Eleanor of Aquitaine and used the strength of this position to found the legendary Angevin Empire. Throughout his reign he expanded into France, Scotland, Ireland and Wales, making the House of Plantagenet one of the most powerful dynasties in the world. With this expansion of power came increased pressure for the ruling monarch, as Henry II now had responsibility for an entire empire that he had fought to conquer and maintain. Because of this, in the years leading up to Henry's death there was increased tension over who would inherit his crown. William Marshal had by now rejoined the court and asked King Henry if he could join his eldest son the foremost heir, referred to as 'Young Henry'. The King probably intended that Marshal would restore some calm to the situation between father and son. Despite this 'Young Henry', aged 28 years, continued the rebellion against his father but died of an illness before its conclusion.

Family rows were lethal in those days and with his elder brother dead, Henry's second son turned on his father. The King was retreating to safety during a skirmish when Richard charged at him, but William Marshal saw what was about to happen and killed the horse underneath him, thus allowing Henry II to escape to safety. When the King died despite his rebellion Richard succeeded in 1189, followed by his juvenile brother John in 1199 and William Marshall served them both.

William Marshal killing Richard's horse from underneath him to save the King.

.Aaron the Jew.

A aron was either born in Lincoln or had been living there for some time. During this period Lincoln was a hub in terms of finance and population, second only to London. The wealthiest man in Norman England was Aaron the Jew, who was involved in a variety of economic activities including building projects, trade and managing money. His financial activities first show up in the Pipe Roll (the accounts of the national exchequer). During the 12th year of Henry II's reign an entry appears in the Pipe Roll of 1165-66 for the County of Lincolnshire. The money sent from the County by the sheriff is entered as "William de Lisle renders count of the ferm of Lincolnshire" (ferm=tax) it then states that it is "By payment by King's writ to Aaron the Jew" This is telling us that this money is paying back a loan from Aaron. Further examination of the Roll uncovers that the same sort of arrangements were made with payments from many other counties. Aaron had an organised banking network on a national and probably international level.

Over his lifetime he acquired a phenomenal amount of wealth that correlated to the whole income of the state for an entire year. Upon his death in 1186 King Henry II was entitled to all of this, and though it was a substantial amount it was nothing compared to the debts and subsequent interest that had been due to Aaron and henceforth the King.

Henry II seized his property as the escheat of a Jewish usurer, and the English crown thus became universal heir to his estate. The actual cash treasure accumulated by Aaron was sent over to France to assist Henry in his war with Philip Augustus, but the vessel containing it went down on the voyage between Shoreham and Dieppe. However, the indebtedness of the smaller barons and knights remained, and fell into the hands of the king to the amount of £15,000, owed by some 430 persons distributed over the English counties. It was for this reason that when the Magna Carta was drawn up, the barons put in the tenth clause that specified when debts to Jews such as Aaron fell into the monarchs hands he was entitled to claim the capitol but not the interest.

The First Barons War (1215-17)

John's rule was characterized by catastrophe, failure and conflict; the Barons War was the culmination of years of discontent among the nobles of England. Within the first five years of his reign the country had witnessed the collapse of the Angevin realm his father had fought tirelessly to build, and the unimaginable loss of Normandy.

King John

Ever since the Norman invasion the following two centuries of Englishmen had viewed the Duchy as their own, therefore its loss to the French was an extreme shock to the people. The next ten years were dominated by conflict with France and failed attempts to win back the lands lost; to finance this John squeezed his Barons and the Church for income tax. The humiliating English defeat at the Battle of Bouvines in 1214 served as the final straw for much of the nobility. In a final attempt to avoid the crisis of civil war between King John and his Barons, a charter was negotiated.

Magna Carta

One of only 4 remaining copies of the original 1215 Magna Carta and the smaller additional Charter of the Forest of 1217 are owned by Lincoln Cathedral and can be seen in the castle.

Perhaps the most influential man under the King of England at this time was William Marshal, Earl of Pembroke, who at the age of 67, was the leading lay negotiator for King John as the charter between the Barons and King John was deliberated. On the 15th of June 1215 what would later become known as the 'Magna Carta' was signed at Runnymede. It was devised to establish the rights of free individuals, the barons and the church, and to limit the powers of the King. The most significant precedent it set was that the monarch could be held accountable to the law just as much as his subjects. Despite this King John did not keep to his word, and in August 1215 Pope Innocent III annulled the charter on the grounds that it had been signed under duress and was therefore illegal.

As head of the Roman Church Pope Innocent III placed a ban on the Church of England celebrating the sacraments after falling out with King John in 1209. The Pope had immense power and eventually King John had to obey his commands and accepts a Lincolnshire Cardinal Archbishop Stephen Langton as Archbishop of Caterbury.

In open rebellion against King John his barons made the extraordinary decision of inviting Prince Louis, heir to the French throne and traditional enemy of England, to invade and take the crown. Louis responded by sailing with his armies and landing in Sandwich on the 22nd of May 1216. This was the catalyst for a rush of royalist desertions and by the summer the majority of the North and East consented to the claim of the French Prince. Crucially, the combined rebel forces held the capitol of London, where Louis was proclaimed king in St Paul's Cathedral. The fortresses of Dover, Windsor, and Lincoln were some of the few strongholds that remained loyal to King John and held out against French forces.

In the autumn of 1216 King John was travelling North towards Lincoln when he fell ill with a fever, and died of dysentery on the 19th of October at Newark.

It had not been a good trip for King John. His entourage split at Kings Lynn, and the larger group rumoured to be carrying vast fortunes of treasure that John had confiscated from monasteries tried to take a short cut across the Wash flood plains. The tide came in and all were lost.

King John and his party took a more comfortable route and it is suspected that the monarch was poisoned on route. By the time he reached Sleaford he was ill, he carried on to Newark Castle where he died.

His nine-year-old son, Henry III, inherited the crown at a critical moment, and without the support of the now seventy-year old William Marshal it is conceivable that a French King would have sat on the English throne. Marshal was appointed as 'Guardian of the Realm', therefore regent until the young king came of age. In an astute attempt to distance Henry from his late fathers despised regime, the Magna Carta was reissued with the smaller Charter of the Forest highlighting the young King's intent to be a just and fair ruler. In response to this a number of the rebellious Barons returned to the royalist cause and declared allegiance to the king.

.The Battle of Lincoln Fair.

In the Spring of 1217 Prince Louis made the strategic decision of splitting his army in two; leading a force to besiege Dover Castle himself, whilst sending a second detachment North to Lincoln, led by Count Thomas of Perche. Due to the death of Gerard of Canville in 1214 the position of constable and protector of Lincoln Castle had reverted to his wife, Lady Nicolaa de la Haye.

The city of Lincoln itself fell quickly to the invading army, but the castle under the control of Lady Nicolaa remained secure and loyal to King Henry. William Marshal recognised that Lincoln Castle was a vital stronghold and could not be allowed to fall to the French. He mustered a force of 400 knights and 250 crossbowmen at Newark, from where they marched by a circuitous route to camp at Stowe, approximately eight miles north-west of Lincoln. Shortly after 6am on Saturday 20th May 1217 the army marched on the city, divided into four divisions led by William Marshal, the Earl of Salisbury, the Earl of Chester and the Bishop of Winchester. Additionally, the mercenary Falkes de Breaute led the force of 250 crossbowmen.

Once alerted of the oncoming attack, the allied French forces holding the city sent a small group to assess the strength of the royalist army in order to form a strategy. Robert Fitz Walter and Saur of Quincy argued that due to their advantage in numbers meeting the inferior force head on in the field offered the best opportunity for victory. Despite this the Count of Perche favoured a defensive strategy, remaining within the city while they continued their assault of the castle and sent men to defend the city gates and battlements. Perche's decision meant that the royalist army had to find a way to force entry into Lincoln. A north-western gate to the city was found barricaded by rubble, and Marshal decided to utilize this as once cleared it would allow a vital unexpected charge into the upper city. To divert the attention of the allied French forces the division led by the Earl of Chester attacked the North Gate to the city now known as the Newport Arch, whilst Falkes de Breaute and his crossbowmen used a postern gate outside the city walls to gain entry to the castle. Once inside the stronghold, they strategically positioned themselves on the ramparts facing the town and rained arrows upon the siege forces. Once the north-western gate to the city was cleared William Marshal's division charged into the city, the French were completely unaware the outer walls had been breached and were therefore taken by surprise. There was intense

Battle of Lincoln Fair (from Matthew Paris's Chronica Majora; circa 1259)

fighting from both sides in the area between the Castle and the Cathedral; it was here that Thomas of Perche was killed by a deadly lance thrust through his eye and into his brain. The death of the rebel forces most prominent figure was a vicious blow to their morale. Royalist forces now pursued them downhill, at this point the North gate was finally breached by the Earl of Chester and his division who joined the internal fray. The entire battle lasted for around 6 hours; but the advantage of having the upper position on the slope meant the final stage of fighting led to a decisive and calculated victory for William Marshal and King Henry III.

Following the battle, the city of Lincoln was plundered by the victorious forces on the pretext that its citizens had supported Louis and his claim to the throne. The many wealthy churches were looted for their gold, silver, ornaments and jewels, and as the clergy had been excommunicated the Cathedral itself was ransacked. The poor folk of the town were targeted despite their weakness, houses were pillaged then set alight and many citizens fled in terror on the River Witham. It is recorded that some drowned in their haste due to the weight in their small boats. For this reason, the battle is sometimes referred to as the 'Battle of Lincoln Fair', as in the wake of their destruction the royalist forces made merry and celebrated their victory.

During this period, the English were constantly at war with the French, and the outcome of this battle reflects that the people who suffered most were the common folk, innocent of any part in the conflict. The average battered citizen could barely tell one soldier from the other, and yet they were punished by all.

Illuatration of the Battle of Lincoln an intense and gruesome battle.

The contemporary chronicler, Roger of Wendover, described the pillaging of Lincoln by the king's soldiers after the battle.

"After the battle was thus ended, the King's soldiers found in the city the waggons of the barons and the French, with the sumpter-horses, loaded with baggage, silver vessels, and various kinds of furniture and utensils, all which fell into their possession without opposition. Having then plundered the whole city to the last farthing, they next pillaged the churches throughout the city, and broke open the chests and store-rooms with axes and hammers, seizing on the gold and silver in them, clothes of all colours, women's ornaments, gold rings, goblets, and jewels. Nor did the Cathedral church escape this destruction, but underwent the same punishment as the rest, for the legate had given orders to the knights to treat all the clergy as excommunicated men, inasmuch as they had been enemies to the church of Rome and to the king of England from the commencement of the war; Geoffrey de Drepinges precentor of this church, lost eleven thousand marks of silver. When they had thus seized on every kind of property, so that nothing remained in any corner of the houses, they each returned to their lords as rich men, and peace with king Henry having been declared by all throughout the city, they ate and drank amidst mirth and festivity. This battle, which, in derision of Louis and the barons, they called " The Fair," ….. Many of the women of the city were drowned in the river, for, to avoid insult, they took to small boats with their children., female servants, and household property, and perished on their journey ; but there were afterwards found in the river by the searchers, goblets of silver, and many other articles of great benefit to the finders ; for the boats were overloaded, and the women not knowing how to manage the boats, all perished, for business done in haste is always badly done.

This was the second time that the ordinary inhabitants of Lincoln had seen their City ravished in 76 years

Following an offer of amnesty from the guardian of the realm, William Marshal, many of the captured rebellious barons switched their allegiance to the true King Henry III. A large portion of the French forces were taken prisoners, including 300 knights and countless foot soldiers. Despite this there are only three recorded deaths. The most notable, Thomas Count of Perche, was buried outside the city in the orchard of a hospital. A knight of Falkes de Breaute's detachment named Reginald Crocus was buried in the monastery at Croxton, and an unknown soldier of the Baron's army was buried outside Lincoln at the meeting of four roads, meaning he was excommunicated. Some knights did manage to escape and reach Prince Louis at London, where they did not receive a kind welcome due to the shame of their flight.

Allegedly William Marshal made over 1000 marks, the modern equivalent of £6,660,000, from the ransom of the great Northern Baron Nicholas I de Stuteville whom he had captured at the battle.

The bulk of the Anglo-French army were crushed at Lincoln; the battle was an extreme turning point of the civil war in the royalist favour. Later that year the French reinforcements were defeated at the Battle of Sandwich, and following this Prince Louis formally renounced his claim to the English throne. Despite not being as well-known as other significant battles, had the outcome been different it is likely a French King would have ruled England.

Following peace with the French, King Henry signed the Charter of the Forest in 1217, which extended liberties and rights to the common man related to using forest land which belonged to the crown. This was significant as royal forests were an important source of fuel, pasture lands, firewood and many more resources. It freed up lands that had become increasingly restricted under King John's rule, and signalled King Henry's intention to set himself apart from his father.

The conflict with the Barons was initiated by an incompetent and selfish King, and ended under the rule of his just son, guided by the pragmatic William Marshal, who had grown from small beginnings to influence English politics and save the English crown from ruin.

William Marshal was invested into the order of the Knight's Templar on his death bed. He died on May 14th 1219 aged 73 years, he is buried in the Temple Church, London.

The tomb of William Marshal, Earl of Pembroke lies within the Temple Church, London.

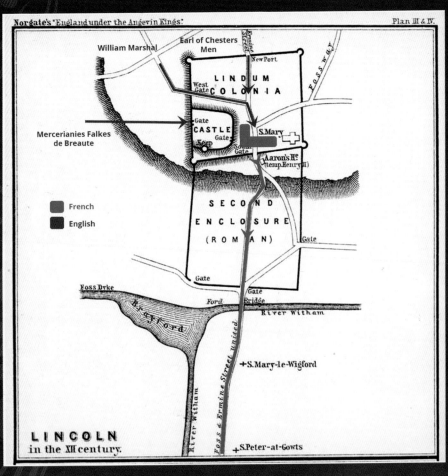

Lincoln as it was in the 12th century showing how the English confronted the French who continued to lay seige at the castle.